MY FAMILY'S SECRET KITCHEN

Traditional Recipes from a North Indian Family Kitchen

To Helen
Happy Cooking
Kumkum

By Mrs Kumkum Chandra

This book is dedicated to my Amma (mother), who encouraged and guided me from my childhood to develop the interest in cooking. Some of these family recipes were lovingly set out in letters from India over the years. She is the reason I have been able to write this book.

Thanks...

To the many people who have helped to make this book possible... but most of all my daughter Monika and my son-in-law Len, who have been behind me without fail from the very beginning.

To my dear husband, Umesh for his support. Without him it would not have been possible.

To my daughter Malini, son Manik, daughter-in-law Lizzie and my family for encouraging me to pass our family recipes to others.

To my grandchildren Kyra, Jasmine, Kiran and Tia who love to learn the tricks of my cooking.

To Martin for his editing skills, Steven and Paul for their design, Charlie for her fantastic photography, Karen for her great writing and also thanks to all the many other people involved but not mentioned above.

Contents

Introduction

by Kumkum Chandra

The concept of a cookbook is strange to me, as I doubt I've ever followed a recipe in my life. My mother taught me how to make these dishes which I subtly altered over time to suit my own palate. Home cooking in India is very much about learning at your mother's knee. From a young age, I could prepare a family meal – although I often managed to burn the dal...

I've passed my methods on in this country by teaching Indian cookery classes and giving demonstrations. Over the past 30 years, people have asked me to write a cookbook and 'share my secrets'. I thought it would be easy to get everything down on paper, but I quickly discovered that cooking is much simpler than writing about it. Simplicity is a guiding principle of my recipes. I don't believe you need a store cupboard full of ingredients to prepare a great tasting meal. In India, most households will have some boiled potatoes ready in the fridge and some spices at hand, which is all they need to produce a tasty curry, served of course with Puri and raita.

Historically in India, it was impossible to keep food fresh so everything was cooked from scratch, three times a day or even more often if unexpected visitors turned up. Making tasty food quickly was a skill all housewives had to perfect. Even today, I make sure I have food prepared and ready to cook, as well as chutneys and pickles that are easy to make and add so much flavour to a simple dish.

My book concentrates on food from my home region of Uttar Pradesh. This northern province is the birthplace of samosas and pakories, the most popular national snacks. It's also famous for biryanis, split dal and khichari. There's nothing complicated about the cooking. The appearance and taste all come from the spices you use, preferably freshly roasted and crushed. Each dish has a different ratio of spices, which is how you create variety. I would advise throwing out the curry powder and following the example of generations of Indians and having a 'curry tin' filled with little pots of spices you can use in varying quantities.

Like me, you'll discover how to play around with ingredients to achieve the best results for you. Cooking Indian food is about experimentation and developing a dish to suit your own taste. My recipes are a guide or an inspiration to get you started. After that, you can evolve your own style and one day pass on your cooking secrets to your friends and family.

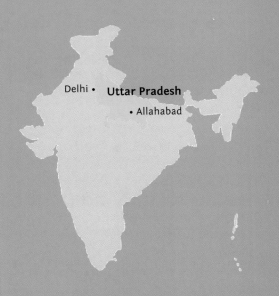

My Cooking Life

In the foothills of Northern India every 12 years something magical happens. Pilgrims from all over the world congregate on Allahabad to bathe in spiritual waters where three holy rivers, the Ganges, Yamuna and mystical Saraswati converge. All Indians try to go to a Kumbh Mela in one of the four locations it takes place at least once in their lifetime. For me, it was easy: I was brought up within reach of one of the sacred sites. While people flocked to Allahabad, I moved away and took with me something else for which the region's famous: the recipes for its exquisite local cuisine.

I was brought up on the specialities of the area like Biryani,

split dal and pulao rice and puris. In times of celebration and holy feasts, we ate puffed rice, sweet poppadoms and dumplings made with dried milk. I often took over at the kitchen stove from my mother when she was ill. It was never a chore for me. I chose to do the cooking, while my sister preferred to clean the house. I hold the same preference to this day!

Food played a huge part in my upbringing. With a vast extended family, many of who would pile up to our house without warning at any time of the day, there was always something being prepared or cooked. As I learnt to make each dish, it stuck in my memory. Recipes were passed down to me like the stories and traditions of my Hindu culture. The recipes I most want to share are for the dishes that have fed my family for generations and which I'm still pleaded to prepare by my own children and grandchildren.
We moved to England in 1971, when my husband got a job as a doctor in

Rotherham. Sometimes I struggled to cook the authentic food of my home region. There was only one shop in Sheffield that sold some of the ingredients so I learned to compromise and started to cook some English dishes. I even began eating beef, which I'd never had before. Of course, in India cows are considered sacred. We call them 'Gaumata' or mother cow because they provide everything for the family. The ox works the land, the cow's milk is used for dairy products including paneer, lassi and ghee, urine is a vital ingredient in many medicines and cow dung mixed with hay provides fuel. If you give a cow to a poor man, it means he can live. I reasoned that the cows here weren't Indian cows so it was all right to eat beef. At that time I made a recipe book of typical dishes from here for people back home. Things like baked potatoes, chicken with mushrooms and Yorkshire puddings were unfamiliar to Indians.

I loved England from the moment I arrived. It was early December and all the streets and shops were ablaze with fairy lights. I remember naively believing that I'd come to a country where they had decorations up all year round. I quickly settled into life here with the help of evening classes. Although I'd been doing research work in zoology in India, I was always happier doing something creative so I took up flower arranging and upholstery and gained qualifications in both. I soon realised there was an opportunity for me at

college to teach Indian cookery and when I started my first course I was overwhelmed by the level of interest and delighted by the diversity of people who turned up. Not only were there English people keen to extend their repertoire, but also Indian people like the man who cooked in a takeaway and had come to learn 'real Indian cooking'. Another memorable student was the long distance lorry driver who revealed how he shunned greasy spoon cafes on his trips, instead packing up homemade Indian soups and pakoris. Most English people then hadn't experienced true Indian food and some had negative preconceptions. One lady at a demonstration absolutely refused to eat anything until I coaxed her to try some of my chicken and rice. I think she surprised herself by having second helpings; she then asked me for my recipes.

In Britain until fairly recently, Indian food has been generic and highly spiced with lots of heat. This isn't the way typical Indian fare is made. My cooking is pared down but flavoursome; each dish speaks for itself. The best way of eating Indian food is to produce a range of small dishes representing an assortment of flavours. I hope you will have fun cooking and eating my selection of recipes. For me, cooking is all about enjoyment and giving, whether to others or myself. So when I'm asked what my secret ingredient is, I always reply 'it's love'.

Kitchen talk

People ask me what I do. The answer is always the same;
"I entertain people with my talks and win their hearts with my food".
Likewise when anyone asks what is the main ingredient in my dishes – I answer "love".

"Nani, please don't die; I will miss your chicken and rice!" – A vote of confidence from my Grand-daughter

I was washing the rice and a voice says; "Let me massage the rice!" – my grand-daughter again.

Compliment from a friend; "you are the best cook in the world... except for my wife of course".

My chief taster is my husband Umesh. If he doesn't like a dish, a polite request follows; "Please don't make that one again".

I asked one of my cookery students what he did. "I work in an Indian restaurant" he replied. "So why are you here?" I said, puzzled. "Because I want to learn how to cook Indian food properly".

After 13 years abroad my friend's daughter came back to England. She came over to visit me. "I am a vegetarian now, auntie. But I would like to have chicken today – I can still remember how good your chicken curry tastes."

Quick Hints

Throw away your curry powder!
If you use the same proportions of spices each dish will taste the same.

My recipes have different combinations of spices to give a wide variety of flavours.

Indian dishes used to be cooked in ghee (clarified butter) or mustard oil. But for health reasons now it is better to use sunflower oil.

If a dish is too spicy (chilli) add one tablespoon of yogurt.

If a dish is too salty add one tablespoon of chopped tomatoes.

Always boil potatoes in their skins then peel them. I use red potatoes in my cooking. Don't add milk or butter when you mash.

Garlic and ginger can be peeled and chopped and put in the freezer in ice cube trays until required.

Disasters

In India everyone sleeps in the afternoon. I used to use that time to cook to please my Amma (mother). One day I decided to make something sweet. As I tipped the ghee tin the lid came loose and the ghee spilt all over the floor. Quickly I grabbed a cloth and mopped up the ghee, and hung the cloth in a corner. I finished making the sweet and went to lie down. After a while I heard Amma shouting me. It was a hot day and the ghee had melted in the cloth and the floor was back in its previous state. Luckily, my sweet was so good that my mother let me off, and encouraged my afternoon experiments.

The Indian Approach to food

In India most people eat 4 times a day:

Breakfast:
Nowadays most people prefer a breakfast of egg and toast, cereal, milk, fruit juice or fruit. The typical Indian breakfast traditionally consists of paratha, 1 vegetable dish or egg bhujiya (scrambled egg), milk and fruit.

Lunch:
At work people have a packed lunch; an Indian packed lunch is chapatti, dal, 1 vegetable, raita and pickle. At home people will commonly tuck into chapatti, a couple of vegetables, dal, raita, rice, salad and something sweet.

Teatime:
Around 4 or 5pm a pot of tea is served with pakoris, samosa and sweets.

Dinner:
Most people sit down to dinner around 8.30-9pm. They will typically have paratha, two vegetables, meat and salad, followed by a sweet. Many people now have chapatti and dal rather than fried parathas or puris.

Planning your menu

A little forethought goes a long way. Try to cook dishes which contrast in colour, texture and taste. This allows you to distinguish the flavour of each dish.

A few do's and don'ts about menus

DON'T serve Milijuli Subji and Bhindi Masala does not go in one menu – it's a collision of spices. But pattabobhi-zeera aloo are fine with them.
DO serve dal, which goes with every dish – it's an ideal accompaniment without strong spicy flavours
DO try the following together; Sag gosht and Khare masala kamurg. Dulma and Shahimurg.
DON'T put Methi aur machli with Sag gosth – they both use leafy vegetables.
DO remember Murg Biryani goes with Rasa and Podine ka raita, Subji Pulao goes with Rasa and Dhania, podina chutney and Plain yogurt.
DO try Matar Pulao for party. It's better than boiled rice and it can be served with any dish.
DO sample Kachoomer if you're looking for a healthy accompaniment. It is an Indian salad and can go with every dish.

Pyaza Pakori

100g sifted gram flour
Teaspoon salt
Teaspoon bicarbonate
  of soda
Teaspoon chilli powder
1 teaspoon crushed
  coriander seeds
1 tablespoon lemon juice
300g large spring onions,
  chopped
Water to make a
  thick paste
Oil for deep frying

Also known as Bhajis. These are great on a rainy day. These are usually served at tea time with a nice cup of tea. The most popular are onion or potato pakoris, as these two ingredients are always found in an Indian kitchen. I often get a migraine when cutting onions and so I tend to use Pyaza (large spring onions).

1. Mix the flour, salt, bicarbonate of soda, chilli powder, coriander seeds and lemon juice into a large bowl.
2. Add water gradually and mix well, making a thick batter. Allow to rest for a few minutes and then mix again.
3. Add the chopped onions and mix.
4. Heat the oil in a pan on medium heat.
5. Fry dumpling size portions of the mixture in the oil.
6. Turn the dumplings over and press so that they cook in the middle.
7. Remove and drain on a piece of kitchen roll when golden brown.
8. Serve with salad, raita and chutney.

Bakcha (Pea Pakora)

80g Gram flour (Baisan)
250g frozen peas
½ teaspoon salt
¼ teaspoon baking powder
½ teaspoon chilli powder
1 tablespoon lemon juice
Water to make a thick
    paste
Oil for deep frying

This is not a very well-known Indian dish, at least in England. But it's one of my family's favourites, and I now share it with you.

1. Mix the flour, salt, bicarbonate of soda, chilli powder, coriander seeds and lemon juice into a large bowl.
2. Add water gradually and mix well, making a thick batter. Allow to rest for a few minutes and then mix again.
3. Add the peas and mix well.
4. Heat the oil in a pan on medium heat.
5. Fry dumpling-size portions of the mixture in the oil.
6. Turn the dumplings over and press so that they cook in the middle.
7. Remove and drain on a piece of kitchen roll when golden brown.
8. Serve with salad, raita or tomato sauce.

Harebhare Kabab (Vegetarian)

1 large potato, boiled
100g frozen spinach, chopped
50g methi (fenugreek) leaves, chopped – if this is unavailable you can use coriander.
1 small red onion, chopped
1 small green chilli, chopped
2.5cm fresh ginger, chopped
1 slice brown or white bread, chopped
1 teaspoon garam masala powder
½ teaspoon chilli powder
Breadcrumbs
Cocktail sticks

Fabulous vegetarian delight.

1. Mash the potato.
2. Combine it with all the other ingredients except the breadcrumbs.
3. Mould the mixture into oval shapes and insert a cocktail stick.
4. Roll the ovals in the breadcrumbs.
5. Warm the griddle and add a little oil.
6. Cook the kababs 3 or 4 at a time until golden brown, turning occasionally and brushing with a little oil.
7. Serve warm with chutney or tomato sauce.

Tandoori Gosht Tikka

650g boneless lamb pieces
2 tablespoons mint leaves
4 tablespoons coriander
leaves
1 small onion, chopped
2.5cm piece of fresh ginger,
chopped
4 cloves of fresh garlic,
chopped
½ green chilli (optional)
¼ teaspoon red chilli
1 teaspoon garam masala
5 almonds (optional)
5 cashew nuts (optional)
6 sultanas (optional)
2 tablespoons yogurt
½ teaspoon meat
tenderiser
1 tablespoon oil
1 teaspoon salt or to taste

Succulent lamb pieces coated with yogurt and roasted until crisp on the outside.

1. Add the meat tenderiser with the lamb and set aside.
2. Make a paste with all the remaining ingredients.
3. Add the lamb and leave for a couple of hours, overnight would be ideal.
4. Heat oven to gas mark 5 or 140°C
5. Place the lamb into a baking dish and cover dish with foil.
6. Cook for 30 minutes.
7. Uncover dish, turn the lamb, leave uncovered and continue to cook until the lamb is cooked.
8. Serve with salad and raita.

Please note this recipe contains nuts.

Tandoori Machli (Tandoori Fish)

450g cod or rainbow trout,
  cut into 2.5cm pieces
3 tablespoons yogurt
3 tablespoons tandoori
  masala powder
3 tablespoons gram flour
1 teaspoon salt or to taste
Oil for frying

Number one for the
whole family. Great as
a pitta pocket filler!

1. Wash the fish pieces and
  set aside.
2. Mix all the remaining
  ingredients in a large
  bowl.
3. Add the fish, mix well
  and leave to marinate
  for 30 minutes.
4. Heat some oil in a
  frying pan. Cook the
  fish, turning once until
  it is cooked through and
  has turned golden
  brown.
5. Serve warm with salad
  and lemon wedges.

Galouti Kabab (Soft Lamb Kabab)

500g lamb, finally minced
2 teaspoons meat
 tenderiser
3 tablespoons gram flour
1 black cardamom
4 black cloves
4 green cardamoms
2 bay leaves
2cm piece of ginger
40g red onion, chopped
2 tablespoons poppy seeds
1 tablespoon grated
 coconut
½ teaspoon chilli powder
1 teaspoon salt or to taste
Oil for brushing

Another dish from Uttar Pradesh – and another legend to go with it.
The story goes that the Mughals – as the local aristocracy of the region really enjoyed eating kababs, but over time they began to have problems with their teeth. (I suspect they were grinding them in their sleep, worrying about being down to their last half a ton of gold and jewels). So they asked their chef to make soft kababs and the Galouti kabab was born. Traditionally raw papaya was used to help tenderise the meat but it is not readily available here so we use a meat tenderiser.

1. Roast the gram flour in a frying pan till you can smell it, put to one side.
2. Grind all the remaining ingredients (except the mince) into a fine paste with a little water.
3. Mix the paste, gram flour, meat tenderiser into a large bowl.
4. Add the mince and leave for at least 3 hours – overnight in the fridge would be fine.
5. Mix again, then place a little oil on the palms of your hands and make small patties with the mince mixture.
6. Put in a dish and microwave for 30 seconds to 1 minute (It makes the kabab softer).
7. Heat a frying pan or tawa and brush with a little oil. Fry the patties, 2 or 3 at a time, for about 30 seconds each side.
8. When golden brown, serve hot with salad and chutney.

The kababs can be prepared the day before and kept in the fridge. Then just complete the final stage of frying when you are ready to serve them.

Jhatpat Murg Tikka
(Quick Chicken Tikka)

500g boneless chicken
  pieces (thigh or breast
  meat), cut into 2cm
  pieces

Paneer (Indian cheese) or
  tofu can also be used as
  a vegetarian alternative

2cm piece of fresh ginger,
  grind into a paste with
  the garlic

4 fresh cloves garlic,
  ground into a paste with
  the ginger

2 teaspoon cumin powder

1 teaspoon crushed
  black pepper

1 teaspoon salt or to taste

1 teaspoon vinegar

1 tablespoon lemon juice

2 tablespoons oil

ADDITIONAL INGREDIENTS
  FOR MAKING KABAB

2 fresh tomatoes,
  cut into 2cm cubes

1 green pepper,
  cut into 2cm cubes

1 yellow pepper,
  cut into 2cm cubes

1 medium onion,
  cut into 2cm cubes

Wooden skewers (*Tip:* soak
  in water for 10 minutes,
  so they don't burn)

1. Wash the chicken and set aside.
2. Mix together all the other ingredients in a large bowl.
3. Add the chicken pieces and leave to marinate for
   15 minutes.
4. Make up the kabab on the skewer using the chicken,
   peppers, onion and tomato.
5. Heat a griddle, brushing with oil or heat 1 tablespoon
   oil in a frying pan.
6. Place the kabab on the griddle or in pan and cook,
   turning occasionally, until the chicken is cooked
   through and has turned a nice golden brown colour.
7. Serve warm with mint raita.
8. Alternatively serve in a roti wrap with salad and raita.

Reshmi Kabab (Soft Chicken Kabab)

650g minced chicken
10 cashew nuts (optional)
3 tablespoon coriander
    leaves
2.5cm piece of fresh ginger
3 cloves of garlic
1 small red onion
1 teaspoon cumin powder
1 teaspoon garam masala
1 teaspoon white pepper
    powder
½ teaspoon meat
    tenderiser
1 egg, beaten
1 teaspoon salt or to taste
Wooden skewers

A speciality of Utter Pradesh. 'Reshmi' means silk – and that beautifully sums up the texture of this kabab.

1. Make a paste with the coriander leaves, ginger, garlic, onion, cashew nuts, cumin powder, garam masala and white pepper powder.
2. Place the paste in a bowl. Pour in the beaten egg and mix well.
3. Add the chicken mince, mix well and leave for between 10-30 minutes or overnight.
4. Using slightly wet hands, wrap the mixture around the skewer and smooth the surface.
5. Brown under a pre-heated grill, turning occasionally, until golden brown.
6. Serve warm with salad and lemon.

Dal Soup

2 sticks celery
1 carrot
¼ small cabbage
2 leeks
3 tomatoes
100g moong dal (split
   green lentils, available
   at supermarkets)
1 teaspoon garam masala
1 teaspoon salt or to taste
Black pepper to taste
1 tablespoon double cream

When I was young, soup was something you served up on a cold day or it was for people who were ill. These days it's very popular both as an everyday meal and also at parties. There's something so satisfying and sustaining about it – one man at my cookery class even told me he always took a flask of my dal soup and some onion pakoris on his long distance trips.

1. Cut all the vegetables into small pieces and sprinkle with salt.
2. Boil all the vegetables and the dal in 600ml of water until the dal is cooked, or cook in a pressure cooker for 5 minutes.
3. Liquidise the cooked mixture.
4. Add the garam masala and pepper to taste, mix well.
5. Serve hot with a tablespoon of cream on top.

Note: Meat stock can be used instead of water.

Sag Gosht (Meat With Spinach)

Serves 4

650g lean lamb (or meat of your choice, soya chunks can also be used), cut into bite size pieces.

175g onion, finely chopped

225g tinned peeled tomatoes

6 tablespoons cooking oil

1 packet of frozen spinach or 450g tin of spinach

1 tablespoon chilli powder

1 teaspoon turmeric powder

2 teaspoons garam masala

2 tablespoons coriander powder

6 cloves of fresh garlic and 1cm fresh ginger, crushed and mixed together

2 teaspoons salt

My children have always loved this. They used to stand near the cooker with plates asking for sag gosht and rice like Oliver asking for seconds or Tom and Jerry in the cartoons

1. Heat the oil in a pan and fry onion until golden brown.
2. Add all the spices, garlic and ginger, and continue frying for 1 minute.
3. Add the tinned tomatoes and fry for further 2 minutes.
4. Add the spinach; continue frying until the oil separates.
5. Add the chopped meat, cover and continue cooking until meat is tender.
6. Serve with rice, chappati or paratha.

Shahi Murg

Serves 4

600g Chicken drumsticks, skinned and washed

1 small onion, finely chopped

1cm piece of fresh ginger, finely chopped

3 cloves of fresh garlic, finely chopped

1 teaspoon chilli powder

1.5 teaspoons garam masala

1 teaspoon coriander powder

1.5 tablespoons tomato purée

1 teaspoon salt or to taste

2 tablespoons oil

125ml double cream

50ml single cream

A rich creamy texture fit for a king

1. Heat the oil in a saucepan.
2. Add the onion and fry until golden brown.
3. Add the garlic and ginger and fry for half a minute.
4. Add the chilli powder, garam masala, coriander powder, salt and tomato purée and fry until you see the oil.
5. Add the chicken pieces and fry until you see the oil.
6. Lower the heat and simmer for about 10 minutes or until the chicken is tender.
7. Add the double and single cream and allow the cream to just heat through.
8. Serve with rice.
9. Garnish with fresh coriander leaves.

Roz Marra Ka Masala (Basic Curry)

Serves 4

150g onion, finely chopped
4 teaspoons coriander
  powder
½ teaspoon turmeric
  powder
1 teaspoon chilli powder
3 teaspoons garam masala
4 cloves fresh garlic, finely
  chopped
2.5cm fresh ginger, finely
  chopped
1 teaspoon paprika powder
200g chopped tomatoes
1 tablespoon green
  coriander leaves,
  chopped
2 teaspoons salt
425ml water
3 tablespoons oil

Master this recipe and an almost endless array of opportunities open up. This basic curry is easy to make because of the limited spices used. But as for what you can create from it, take your pick – it's equally good with chicken, potato, cauliflower or a combination of vegetables.

1. Heat the oil in a saucepan.
2. Fry the chopped onion until golden brown.
3. Add the chopped garlic and ginger and fry for 2 minutes.
4. Add the coriander powder, turmeric, chilli, paprika, salt and 1 teaspoon garam masala and fry for 2 minutes.
5. Add the tomatoes and fry until the oil separates. Add your chosen main ingredient to the masala. (I have used a full small chicken, cut into small pieces).
6. Fry on a high heat until the oil separates (about 10 minutes). The more you fry in the masala the tastier the dish.
1. Pour in the water and cook on low heat until your chosen main ingredient is tender.
2. Add 2 teaspoons garam masala.
3. Finish with the chopped coriander leaves.
4. Serve with rice or chappati.

Kaliya

650g meat(lamb or other
  meat), cut into small
  pieces
115g onion, grated
1cm fresh ginger,
  finely chopped
10 cloves fresh garlic,
  finely chopped
3 red chillies, finely
  chopped (optional)
½ teaspoon turmeric
  powder
½ teaspoon chilli powder
1 teaspoon poppy seeds
2 teaspoons coriander
  powder
150ml water
6 green cardamom pods
  (2 for dry roasting,
  4 crushed)
1 teaspoon cumin seeds
6 whole cloves
12 black peppercorns
15g flaked or crushed
  almonds (optional)
150ml natural yogurt
1 teaspoon salt or to taste
Pinch of grated nutmeg
2 tablespoon tomato purée
2 teaspoons garam masala
5 tablespoons oil

Kaliya is a dish traditionally made with mutton. It has a gravy and it is essential to include turmeric or saffron when cooking as it enhances the colour of the dish.

1. Heat 2 tablespoons of oil in a pan.
2. Add the meat and fry until golden brown, remove from the pan and set aside.
3. Dry roast the poppy seeds, cumin seeds, almonds, 2 green cardamom pods, peppercorns, cloves, nutmeg.
4. Grind the dry roasted spices together with the fresh ginger, garlic and red chillies to form a paste.
5. Add 3 tablespoons of oil in a pan, add the crushed green cardamom pods and grated onion and fry until golden brown.
6. Add the chilli powder, turmeric and the mixed spice paste and continue frying for 2 minutes.
7. Beat the yogurt into the pan mixture, add the tomato purée and continue cooking for 3 minutes.
8. Add the browned meat and salt and cook until the oil starts to separate from the mixture
9. Add the water and cover and cook until the meat is tender. Finally add the garam masala, garnish with fresh coriander.
10. Serve with tandoori roti.

Dulma (Minced Meat With Peas)

Serves 4

650g minced lamb (soya mince can be used)

4 cloves of fresh garlic, finely chopped

1 large onion, finely chopped

4cm piece fresh ginger, finely chopped

100ml oil

2 tablespoons coriander powder

1 teaspoon chilli powder

2 teaspoon garam masala

1 teaspoon turmeric powder

125ml tinned chopped tomato

125g frozen peas

1 tablespoon tomato purée

1 teaspoon salt

1 tablespoon freshly chopped coriander leaves

Whole spices:

2.5cm stick of cinnamon

4 whole cloves

4 peppercorns

2 green cardamom pods

1 teaspoon cumin

2 bay leaves

1. Heat the oil in a saucepan and fry all the whole spices.
2. Add the ginger, onion and garlic and fry until golden brown.
3. Add the minced meat and fry for 3-4 minutes, season with salt and continue frying. Put the spices in the pan one by one and continue frying on a low heat. (use only 1 teaspoon of the garam masala at this point)
4. Stir in the tomato purée and chopped tomato.
5. Continue frying until the oil separates and then add the peas.
6. Continue cooking on a low heat, until the meat is cooked, stirring occasionally.
7. Sprinkle in the remaining garam masala and chopped coriander leaves.
8. Serve with paratha or roti.

This dish is best served dry but if you would prefer some gravy just add a little water.

Khara Masala Ka Murg

600g boneless chicken
  thighs or breast pieces,
  skinless and cut into
  3cm pieces.
1 small onion,
  finely chopped
2cm fresh ginger,
  roughly chopped
2 cloves fresh garlic,
  roughly chopped
1 medium fresh tomato,
  chopped
2 bay leaves
2 green cardamom pods
4 black peppercorns
4 cloves
½ teaspoon nutmeg
  powder
½ teaspoon mace powder
1 teaspoon cumin seeds
2cm long cinnamon stick
1 teaspoon crushed
  coriander seeds
1 teaspoon chilli powder
1 teaspoon salt or to taste
2 tablespoons oil
2 tablespoons natural
  yogurt

Chicken with whole spices. For a vegetarian version, Indian cheese (paneer) or tofu can be used instead.

1. Mix together the yogurt and the salt in a large bowl.
2. Add the chicken pieces and marinate for 15–30 minutes
3. Heat the oil in a saucepan.
4. Add the bay leaves, green cardamom pods, black peppercorns, cloves, nutmeg powder, mace powder, cumin seeds, cinnamon stick, crushed coriander seeds and chilli powder.
5. Add the onion and fry until soft and light brown.
6. Add the garlic and ginger and fry for 30 seconds.
7. Add the marinated chicken and fry until you see the oil.
8. Add the chopped tomato and cook for a few minutes until the chicken is tender, and half the liquid is absorbed
9. Serve with paratha, roti or tandoori roti.

Rara Gosht

500g lamb pieces, cut into 2cm cubes
250g chicken mince
2 bay leaves
1 black cardamom
3 green cardamoms
4 teaspoons coriander powder
1 teaspoon cumin powder
½ teaspoon chilli powder
½ teaspoon turmeric powder
2 cm fresh ginger, finely chopped
4 fresh cloves garlic, finely chopped
150g onion, finely chopped
120g chopped tinned tomatoes
50g plain yogurt
Salt to taste
3 tablespoon oil
3 tablespoons water
3 tablespoons fresh coriander leaves, chopped

This is a mixture of lamb and chicken in a spicy masala. It may sound like an unlikely combination but it is a sumptuous pairing!

This dish is normally served quite dry but just pour in some more water if you'd like more sauce.

If you want a hotter curry, add some chopped green chillies.

1. Whisk together the yogurt and salt and marinade the minced chicken and lamb in the mixture for an hour.
2. Cook the bay leaves and cardamoms in a saucepan until they crackle.
3. Add the onions and fry until light golden brown.
4. Sprinkle in the ginger, garlic, coriander, turmeric and red chilli powder.
5. Tip in the chopped tomatoes and fry until the oil separates from the mixture.
6. Add the marinated lamb and chicken and bring to boil before reducing the heat.
7. Fry until the lamb is tender, slowly adding 3 tablespoons of water, making sure that the water does not evaporate.
8. Serve with the chopped coriander leaves, paratha, tandoori roti or chapatti.

Machli Aur Methi
(Fish Cooked In Fenugreek Leaves)

600g cod fillets, skinned
  and cut into 5cm pieces
1 small onion, finely
  chopped
1cm piece of fresh ginger,
  finely chopped
3 cloves garlic, finely
  chopped
½ teaspoon turmeric
  powder
1 teaspoon cumin powder
1 teaspoon coriander
  powder
½ teaspoon chilli powder
1 teaspoon garam masala
1 teaspoon yellow mustard
  seeds or dijon mustard
2 tablespoons dried or 1
  cup fresh fenugreek
  leaves
2 medium fresh tomatoes,
  chopped
1 teaspoon salt or to taste
4 tablespoons oil

1. Rub the salt and turmeric over the fish.
2. Heat 2 tablespoons oil in a frying pan.
3. Add the fish and fry for 1 minute each side
   until lightly browned.
4. Remove and drain on kitchen roll.
5. Heat 2 tablespoons of oil in a saucepan.
6. Add the mustard seeds and stir.
7. Add the onions and fry until lightly browned.
8. Add the garlic and ginger and fry for 30 seconds.
9. Add the cumin powder, coriander powder, chilli
   powder and garam masala and fry until absorbed.
10. Add the tomato and fry for 1 minute.
11. Add the fenugreek leaves and fry until you see the oil.
12. Add the fried fish and cook in the sauce, turning once.
13. Add cup of water. Lower heat and simmer for 5–6
    minutes, until the fish is cooked.
14. Serve with boiled rice.

Milijuli Subji Korma

1 small cauliflower
1 medium aubergine
1 red pepper
1 medium courgette
2 carrots
1 small swede
3 tablespoons oil
1 onion, chopped
2.5cm fresh ginger,
   chopped
3 cloves garlic, chopped
2 teaspoons coriander
   powder
1 teaspoon turmeric
   powder
½ teaspoon chilli powder
1 teaspoon garam masala
85g chopped tinned
   tomatoes
Salt to taste
150ml water
3 tablespoons double or
   sour cream (optional)

An amazing combination of colour and taste

1. Fry the onion in the oil until golden brown.
2. Add the garlic and ginger and cook for 30 seconds,
   then sprinkle in the remaining spices, frying for a
   further 30 seconds.
3. Drop in the chopped tomatoes and cook for 2 minutes
   before adding the vegetables.
4. Pour in the water and simmer on a moderate heat
   until the vegetables are soft.
5. Stir in the cream and serve hot with rice or chapatti.

Bhindi Masalewali (Okras In Spices)

600g bhindi/okra
130g onion, finely chopped
3 tablespoons oil
2 cloves garlic, chopped
1.5cm fresh ginger, chopped
1 teaspoon turmeric powder
½ teaspoon chilli powder
4 teaspoons coriander powder
2 teaspoons garam masala
1 teaspoon salt or to taste
3 medium fresh tomatoes, chopped

These "ladies' fingers" are so delicate, with a luxurious velvety texture

1. Wash, dry and split the bhindi lengthways, cutting through the flesh about halfway, so that one edge is still intact.
2. Fry the onions in the oil on a medium heat until golden brown.
3. Add the garlic and ginger and fry for 1 minute, then sprinkle in the turmeric, chilli, coriander, garam masala and salt and cook for a further minute.
4. Drop the bhindi into the pan and cook, stirring the mixture 2-3 times.
5. Fry the tomatoes until soft and the mixture becomes fairly dry.
6. Serve with puri, chapatti or paratha.

If too salty, just stir in a little more tomato.

Bhuna Pattaghobhi (Fried Cabbage)

2 small white cabbages,
  roughly chopped
4 cloves of garlic,
  coarsely chopped
1 teaspoon dry crushed
  red chilli
2 tablespoons oil
1 teaspoon salt or to taste

Traditionally a side dish, which should be served alongside dal or a meat main course

1. Heat the oil in a big frying pan and fry the garlic until pink.
2. Add the chilli and cabbage and mix together.
3. Season with salt, cover and cook on a low heat.
4. When the cabbage has started to cook down, turn up the heat and fry until the mixture is dry.

Zeera Ka Aloo (Potato With Cumin)

500g potato with skins
2 tablespoon oil
1 tablespoon zeera/cumin
   seeds
½ teaspoon crushed dry
   red chilli
3 tablespoons chopped
   tomatoes
1 teaspoon salt or to taste
2 tablespoons fresh
   coriander leaves
300ml water

This is a very special dish from Utter Pradesh and great for people who don't eat onion or garlic. Although very plain and simple, it's a very tasty dish and best served with puris. In our family we call this dish Pooja (which means prayer) aloo because we normally serve this dish on prayer days.

1. Boil the potatoes until soft, peel off the skin and break into small pieces.
2. Cook the zeera seeds and when they begin to pop add the chilli, salt, potato and tomatoes.
3. Fry for 2 minutes, pour in 300ml of water and cook on a low heat for 3 minutes.
4. Add the coriander leaves and serve.
5. If you prefer a drier curry don't add the water at stage 3.

Masoor Masala Dal

150g masoor dal
  (red split lentils)
1 small onion, chopped
2 cloves garlic, chopped
1cm fresh ginger, chopped
Half green chilli
3 teaspoons coriander
  powder
½ teaspoon chilli powder
½ teaspoon garam masala
½ teaspoon turmeric
  powder
Salt, to taste
5 tablespoons chopped
  tinned tomatoes
3 tablespoons oil
600ml water

This is a very quick dish made from red lentils. It is one of my father's favourite dishes and he claims it's the best masoor masala ever made!

1. Wash the dal and boil in a saucepan with the other ingredients.
2. Reduce the heat and cook for about 25 minutes, until the dal is soft, stirring continuously.
3. Serve with rice or roti.

Quti Dal
(Split Channa Dal & Split Black Urad Dal)

150g channa dal (split)
150g Split black Urad dal
1 teaspoon turmeric
   powder
1 teaspoon salt
800ml water

FOR TARKA
3 tablespoons ghee or any
   cooking oil
3 cloves garlic, coarsely
   chopped
1 teaspoon Hing
   (asafoetida)
2.5cm fresh ginger,
   coarsely chopped
1 dried red chilli, broken
   into 2 pieces
1 teaspoon crushed chilli

There is an old legend about how this dish – a combination of two types of dal – was created. The story goes that a cantankerous mother-in-law mixed two dals together and asked her daughter-in-law to separate them and cook them separately. She managed this feat much to her mother-in-law's dismay. So a few days later the old lady asked her to do it again. But this time she didn't separate the dals, but went ahead and cooked them together. When it was served to the mother-in-law, she heaped compliments on the girl's marvellous cooking skills and declared it was the finest she had ever tasted. Try it, and you might agree.

1. Wash the dals and place in a saucepan with the turmeric powder and salt. Cover with the water, bring to boil, then reduce to a medium heat until the dal is soft.
2. Make sure that the dal mixture is not too wet. If so, cook it a little longer. Taste and add extra salt if required.
3. Next make the tarka by heating the oil in a pan and frying the hing, garlic and ginger until they are a light pink.
4. Add the dried and crushed chillies.
5. Pour the tarka over the dal and serve with roti.

Arhar Tarka Dal

250g arhar ki dal
  (split pigeon-pea) also
  known as toor dal
½ teaspoon turmeric
1 teaspoon salt or to taste
2 fresh tomatoes, chopped
  or 3 tablespoons
  chopped tinned
  tomatoes.
1½ pint water

TARKA INGREDIENTS
2 tablespoons ghee or
  vegetable oil
2-3 garlic cloves, chopped
1 teaspoon cumin seeds
1 teaspoon mustard seeds
8 curry leaves (optional)
½ teaspoon garam masala
2-3 whole dried chilli
1cm ginger, chopped

Dal is a fundamental part of Indian cuisine – it's rare to find a meal without some on the table. Its rich, savoury taste is best enjoyed when scooped up with a chapatti or other bread.

Of course with a dish that's so universal everyone has a favourite version and this is mine. It found favour with other people as well, as I found out in my student days in Uttar Pradesh. When we used to go to lectures, we would often take this dal in our tiffin boxes, but the visiting students used to steal it from us and leave in its place their own, which wasn't nearly as good.

It's a great choice for vegetarians as it provides them with the protein they require. Ghee is used in this particular recipe to add flavour and a delicious aroma.

1. Wash the dal thoroughly in 2-3 changes of water, drain and place in a saucepan along with the salt, turmeric and chopped tomatoes.
2. Cover with the water and bring to boil.
3. Reduce to low heat and continue to cook for 15-20 minutes until lentils have turned soft and mushy. Place in a serving dish.
4. Melt the ghee in a frying pan over a low heat, then cook the curry leaves, cumin seeds and mustard seeds until they begin to pop.
5. Add the chopped garlic, chopped ginger and whole dried chillies and continue slowly frying until the mixture turns golden brown, and the garlic and ginger pieces become pale pink. Add the garam masala, pour the Tarka over the dal and serve.

Chapattis

250g Chapatti flour
Water

1. Knead the flour and water into a soft dough, leave for 10 minutes then divide into 8–10 dumpling size portions.
2. Roll each piece into a ball between your hands.
3. Using a rolling pin, flatten each ball to into a 20cm diameter circle.
4. Heat a heavy frying pan or tava (an Indian chapatti pan).
5. Lay each portion into the pan and cook until small blisters form on the underside.
6. Flip over, place directly on the gas ring and cook until brown blisters appear and the chapatti is puffed up. If you have an electric cooker, use the heated pan and press down during cooking..

Tandoori Roti

250g Chapatti flour
100ml water
2 tablespoons milk
1 tablespoon water
1 tablespoon oil or ghee

Note: These rotis can be made a day or two in advance(upto step 6). When ready to use, reheat the roti spot side up under the grill and then follow the recipe from step 7.

Traditionally these rotis are cooked in a Tandoor oven, the grill will suffice.

1. Make a soft dough with the flour and water, knead well.
2. Divide the dough into 8 dumpling-size portions.
3. Roll each piece of dough into a ball between your hands.
4. Using a rolling pin, roll each ball into a flat round pancake (about ½cm thick).
5. Heat a heavy frying pan or tava (Indian Chapatti pan).
6. Place the roti into the pan. Cook until brown patches appear. Remove from the pan.
7. Mix together the milk and 1 tablespoon water.
8. Prick the undercooked side of the roti with a fork.
9. Brush this side of the roti with the milk/water mixture. Cook under a pre-heated grill until turning brown.
10. Brush the roti with ghee.
11. Serve hot with dal, vegetables or meat.

Paratha

250g Chapatti flour
Pinch of salt
1 teaspoon oil
Water
2 tablespoons ghee

1. Mix the flour, oil, salt and water together to make a soft dough. Knead well and leave for 10 minutes.
2. Divide the mixture into 8-10 even portions.
3. Roll each ball into a circle, the size of a small plate.
4. Place half a teaspoon of ghee in the centre of the circle and fold it in half.
5. Brush with more ghee and fold again.
6. On a floured surface, roll the folded paratha into a circle again.
7. Heat a tava (heavy pan) and brush with ghee.
8. Cook the paratha on the tava for 30 seconds each side, brushing with ghee, until golden brown.
9. Keep pressing the paratha with a spatula so that it is completely cooked.
10. Place on a piece of kitchen roll to absorb any excess ghee. Serve hot.

Puri

250g Chappati flour
Water to make a
    stiff dough
½ teaspoon salt
1 tablespoon oil
Vegetable oil for frying

1. Mix the flour and water, salt and oil to make a stiff dough. Leave for 10 minutes.
2. Take a piece of dough and roll out into discs about 10cm diameter.
3. Heat the oil in a saucepan, do not start to cook the puris until the oil is nice and hot.
4. Drop each puri into the hot oil, the puri should puff up and cook in about 30 seconds.
5. Using a slotted spoon turn the puri and cook on the other side, again only for about 30 seconds.
6. Lift out the puri and place on a piece of kitchen roll and drain off the excess oil.
7. Serve hot.

Chicken Biryani

10 tablespoon ghee
1½ teaspoon cumin seeds
5cm cinnamon stick
6 cloves
1 teaspoon cardamom
  seeds
2 teaspoons salt
 2 onions, thinly sliced
3 cloves garlic, crushed
4cm piece ginger, crushed
6 peppercorns
1 teaspoon chilli powder
½ teaspoon saffron threads
  soaked in hot water
450g long grain rice
  (Basmati)
 1.3kg chicken, cut into
  small pieces
350ml yogurt
85g almonds (optional)

For the sauce
100ml tomato juice
½ teaspoon chilli powder
1 teaspoon garam masala
1 tablespoon oil
50ml yogurt
1 teaspoon dhania powder
½ teaspoon haldi
1 teaspoon salt or to taste

This dish was traditionally made with mutton. Despite the impression you might get from the menu at some restaurants, chicken was not commonly used in Indian cooking until the early 1950s.

It is prepared by cooking the rice and chicken separately and layering the ingredients.

1. Melt 8 tablespoons of ghee in a large pan. Fry the garlic, ginger, chilli powder and cumin seeds for 3 minutes.
2. Add the chicken and fry until the oil separates from the spice mixture.
3. Place the cinnamon, cloves, peppercorns, cardamoms, yogurt salt in the pan and cook on a low heat until the chicken is tender.
4. Bring 3 pints of water to boil in a large pan with 1 teaspoon salt. Boil the rice for 5-6 minutes until soft. Drain and keep to one side.
5. Pre-heat the oven to gas mark 4.
6. Fry the onion in a little ghee.
7. Melt 2 tablespoons ghee in a large casserole. Place one third of the boiled rice over the bottom of the pan.
8. Next, layer with one third of the chicken mixture and one third of the saffron.
9. Continue to layer with half of the fried onion. Cover with one third of the chicken mixture and one third of the rice. Sprinkle with the saffron mixture.
10. Add the remaining chicken mixture, then layer with rice, saffron water and the remaining onion.
11. Cover the casserole tightly and cook in the oven for 20 minutes.
12. Serve warm with special Biryani sauce.

To make the sauce
1. Heat the oil in a pan, add all the spices and fry for 30 seconds.
2. Add the tomato juice and yogurt, cook for 3 minutes on low heat.

Matar Pulao

350g basmati rice
600ml water
1 teaspoon cumin seeds
1cm cinnamon stick
4 black cloves
4 black peppercorns
2 bay leaves
2 cardamom pods
115g frozen peas
2 tablespoons oil
2 teaspoons salt

This pulao rice with peas is a nice alternative to plain rice and tastes great served with any of my curries.

1. Wash and clean the rice and soak in water.
2. Fry the spices in oil for 30 seconds, then tip in the peas and salt and cook for a further 2 minutes.
3. Add the rice and water, bringing the mix to the boil
4. Turn down the heat and cover, continue cooking until all the water is absorbed and the rice is soft.
5. Stir once or twice and serve.

Tahari (Mixed Vegetable Biryani)

225g basmati rice
115g onion, chopped
3 garlic cloves, chopped
2½cm fresh ginger,
    chopped
2 tablespoons ghee or oil
1 teaspoon black cumin
    seeds
1 teaspoon coriander seeds
5cm cinnamon stick
2 bay leaves
4 black pepper corns
2 green cardamon pods
4 cloves
1 teaspoon turmeric
1 teaspoon garam masala
750ml water
1 teaspoon salt
½ teaspoon chilli powder
175g mixed vegetables
½ a small carton plain
    yogurt

This is a good lazy Sunday meal.

1. Wash the rice well (in at least 5 changes of water and leave aside to soak).
2. Heat the oil and ghee in a pan and add the black cumin, bay leaves, black cardamon pods, green cardamon pods, coriander seeds and cloves and fry until golden brown.
3. Fry the onions, garlic and ginger for 5 minutes, stirring frequently.
4. Stir in the turmeric and chilli powder and cook for 30 seconds. Spoon in the yogurt and mix well.
5. Drop in the vegetables and the salt and cook for 3 minutes.
6. Add the garam masala powder and stir the mixture well, bring the mixture to the boil, cover the pan with a lid and simmer for about 15 minutes or until vegetables are tender, rice cooked and water reduced.
7. Serve warm with biryani sauce (see page 47).

Uble Chaval (Boiled Rice)

250g basmati rice
(the best is grown on
hills of Uttar Pradesh)
900ml cold Water
½ teaspoon lemon juice
(this gives rice a whiter
colour)
½ teaspoon oil (this helps
separate the rice)
A pinch of salt

Rice is a major accompaniment to many Indian dishes. Every region has its own unique way of preparing rice.

When cooking boiled rice it should be light and fluffy, with each and every grain separate. There are a number of factors which contribute to achieving the right effect:

- The type of rice used
- The number of washes
- Time allowed to soak
- The amount of water used

1. Wash the rice and put into a bowl.
2. Add enough water to cover. Rrub the rice (my granddaughter says you have to massage it!) This helps to remove the starch. Repeat this 3 times.
3 Place the rice in a large saucepan with the water, lemon and salt. Allow to rest for 10 minutes.
4 Bring to the boil over a high heat, simmer and cover. Stir once and cook until grains are tender and separate (about 20 minutes).

One food critic asked me how to make boiled rice because her boiled rice ends up as rice pudding!

Tip: I measure the amount of water needed for cooking the rice by placing my index finger so it just rests on top of the rice and the water reaches half way up my finger.

Khichari

150g rice
150g split green moong
   dahl
½ teaspoon hing
   [Asafoetida] powder
1 teaspoon cumin seeds
½ teaspoon chilli powder
1 teaspoon salt or to taste
2 tablespoons oil

If you're not well-versed in the Indian language, this one can catch you out. Khichari can be either a hot and spicy dish of dal and rice flavoured with spices, or a very light mild dish which is ideal when you are not feeling well.

The very similar-sounding Kedgeree is a British adaptation of the original Indian dish. It uses flaked fish and hard-boiled eggs instead of dal and is less spicy. 'Khichari' means four friends and indeed the dish includes four ingredients which blend amicably – Ghee (clarified butter), Dhai (yogurt), Pappad (poppadom) and Achar (pickle).

1. Wash the rice and dal twice and mix together, set aside.
2. Heat the oil in a saucepan.
3. Add the hing, cumin seeds and chilli powder, stir well.
4. Add the rice and dal mixture and fry for 1 minute.
5. Add the salt and 650ml water and bring to a boil.
6. Cover and cook on a low heat until the rice and dahl are soft and cooked and all the liquid is absorbed.
7. Fry some onion and put over the khichari.

Shahi Tukray
(Sweet Indian Bread Pudding)

6 slices of medium
  white bread
170g sugar
200ml water
3 green cardamom seeds,
  without husks
Chopped pistachio nuts
  (optional)
Ghee for frying
  (oil can be used)

Here's a special dessert from Uttar Pradesh.
It is traditionally served to royalty and
therefore is made with many rich ingredients
such as cream, clotted cream, ghee and nuts.
Although I've adapted the following recipe,
it has not lost any of the lovely flavours.

1. Cut each slice of bread into halves.
2. Heat the ghee in a frying pan.
3. Fry the bread slices until they are crisp and
   golden brown.
4. Make a runny syrup with the sugar, water and
   cardamom seeds. Allow to cool.
5. Dip each bread slice into the syrup for 30 seconds.
6. Remove from the syrup and arrange in a dish.
7. Serve warm, with cream and sprinkle with chopped
   pistachio nuts. (Can also be served cold)

Note: This recipe contains nuts

Gajar Ka Halwa (Carrot Halwa)

1.5kg carrots, peeled
  and grated
200ml tinned condensed
  milk (sweetened)
Seeds of 2 green
  cardamoms
75ml ghee (purified butter)
35g blanched almonds,
  chopped (optional)

An Indian meal is never complete without a dessert. Gajar Ka Halwa is a popular rich winter dish throughout the Indian regions. Usually it takes hours to prepare, my quick recipe is a new take on an Indian classic.

1. Cook the grated carrots with the condensed milk on a low heat, stirring continuously, until the carrots are soft and the milk has evaporated.
2. Mix in the cardamom seeds and ghee and cook over a low heat, continuing to stir.
3. The dish will turn a deep red as it cooks and after 20 minutes, the ghee will separate from the mixture.
4. Sprinkle over the almonds and serve, hot or cold.

Hint: Keep stirring throughout the cooking!

Beaje Ki Barfi (Seed Barfi)

250g mixed seeds,
  sunflower, pumpkin
  and pine kernels (seeds
  can be ground)
150g sugar
100ml water

I remember my grandmother and her friends used to peel melon seeds, as you can imagine a slow and tedious process, to make barfi to celebrate the birthday of Rama and Krishna.

As time went on, they didn't need to do this so much, as it was available to buy in the shops. Nowadays, the seeds are readily available and they are all peeled and ready to be cooked with.

Making good barfi comes with experience, so why not give it a go!! Even if it does not set it will still taste delicious!

1. Grease a chopping board with oil.
2. Boil the sugar and water in a pan until thick and sticky, remove from the heat.
3. Add the seeds and mix well, until the mixture begins to thicken.
4. Spread the mixture onto the chopping board, to a thickness of ½cm and press with the back of a cold spoon.
5. Allow the mixture to cool and harden, then cut into squares. (If not set, still taste some!)

Kulfi

600ml milk
200ml condensed milk
1 tablespoon arrowroot or
   cornflour
4 tablespoons pistachios,
   shredded
6-8 strands saffron
   (optional)

Kulfi is made from condensed milk and is denser and creamier than traditional ice-cream – a 'naughty but nice' dessert! Traditionaly Kulfi takes hours to make, this is my quick version.

1. Boil the milk on a low heat until creamy and reduced by half.
2. Dissolve the arrowroot in a little cooled milk and heat until it can be easily poured.
3. Stir in the condensed milk, pistachios and saffron.
4. Whip the mixture, until it is light, fluffy and slightly cooled.
5. Place in the freezer until frozen.
6. Remove from the freezer 5 minutes before serving.

To make mango kulfi:
Use 4 tablespoons of crushed fresh mango or tinned mango slices. Add the mango when the mixture has cooled and whisk.

To make almond kulfi:
Instead of cornflour add 1 tablespoon of almond power and 1 tablespoon of shredded almonds.

Podine Ka Raita (Mint Raita)

1 tablespoon dry or 2
  tablespoons fresh mint,
  chopped
½ teaspoon chilli powder
125ml yogurt
50ml water
Salt to taste

Although this well-known accompaniment contains a hint of chilli, which give it its distinctive flavour, raita is there to have a cooling effect to counter the heat of spicy dishes.

1. Beat the yogurt and water together with a fork.
2. Add the chopped mint, chilli powder and salt. Serve with any dish.

Pyaz Ka Raita (Onion Raita)

1 small onion, chopped
½ teaspoon chilli powder
125ml plain yogurt
50ml water
Salt to taste

Raita is simple to make, a good counter to spicy dishes – and delicious in its own right!

1. Beat the yogurt and water together with a fork.
2. Add the chopped onion, chilli powder and salt. Cool for a short time in the fridge before serving.

Haremirch Ka Achar
(Green Chilli Pickle – Hot)

15 green fresh chillies
2 tablespoons mustard seeds
2 tablespoons lemon juice
Salt to taste

If you prefer a hotter achar simply add more chillies

Quick to prepare, this pickle has a short shelf life. It is a favourite at wedding feasts.

1. Cut the chillies into 1cm pieces.
2. Coarsely grind the mustard seeds.
3. Place both ingredients in a bowl with the chillies, lemon juice and salt.
4. Mix together well and place in a glass container. Leave in a warm place. The achar will be ready in 3-4 days.

Dhania Aur Podina Chutney
(Coriander & Mint Chutney)

½ bunch fresh coriander with stalks
3 tablespoons fresh mint
1 green chilli
1 small cooking apple, peeled and chopped juice of half a lemon
1 teaspoon chat masala
½ teaspoon salt or to taste

Best accompaniment with every dish.

1. Grind all the ingredients together in a pestle and mortar.
2. Add the lemon juice and mix well. The chutney is now ready to serve.
3. To make the chutney sweet add 1 tablespoon of sugar and mix well.

Sweet Imli Ki Chutney
(Sweet Tamarind Chutney)

2 tablespoons
  tamarind paste
1 teaspoon chilli powder
1 teaspoon chaat masala
  (can be bought from
  Asian food stores)
1cm fresh ginger, grated
6 tablespoons sugar
6 tablespoons water
1 teaspoon sultanas
  (optional)

1. Mix all ingredients together, stir and make a smooth paste. Cook for 3 minutes. Chutney will become porridge consistency.
2. Serve as an accompaniment to pakoris.

Poppadoms

These are made from a mixture of various ground lentils and flour which form hard dough. Chillies and spices are added and then the mix is rolled into very thin rounds and allowed to dry. Poppadoms can be cooked in 3 different ways:

Frying method
1. Heat oil in a frying pan and lay a small round in the pan. If it sizzles, temperature is correct.
2. Cook each poppadom separately and cook until they are a pale yellow. This will take a few seconds.
3. Remove and place on absorbent paper.

Grilling method
1. Place the poppadoms under a medium grill, 2-3 inches from the heat source.
2. Grill on both sides until the surface is golden brown.

On the gas stove
1. Pick up a poppadom with tongs and hold 1cm above the gas flame.
2. Turn the poppadom quickly to prevent burning.
3. Keep turning until the whole poppadom is cooked.

Fried Broad Beans

1kg bag of frozen
   broad beans
1 teaspoon chaat
   masala or to taste
Oil for deep frying

Here's a speciality of the town where my family used to live and where I still have some family to this day. This is not a common dish so many people are missing a culinary delight! Although the preparation is tedious the end result is well worth it.

1. Place the broad beans in a large bowl and cover with boiling water.
2. After 6-8 minutes, remove from the water and peel the beans by pressing the outer skin, so the beans split in two.
3. Dry the peeled beans on a piece of kitchen roll.
4. Heat the oil in a pan and deep fry the beans until light brown. Remove and drain on kitchen roll (the beans will crisp up as they cool).
5. Mix the beans with the chaat masala and serve.

If you prefer them crisper, place in a low oven for a few minutes. They're great served with pre-dinner drinks.

Kachoomer

1 medium onion, chopped
2 firm tomatoes, chopped
½ cucumber, cut into
   1cm pieces
2 tablespoons sprouting
   beans (optional can be
   bought from supermarket)
3 tablespoons tinned
   sweetcorn
½ green pepper, cubed
½ red or yellow pepper,
   cubed
2½cm fresh ginger, finely
   chopped
1 green chilli, chopped
   (optional)
2 cloves garlic, finely
   chopped
3 tablespoons lime juice
1 teaspoon salt or to taste
1 tablespoon chaat masala
   (available from Asian food
   stores)
½ teaspoon chilli powder
   (optional)

A tasty salad of onion, tomato and cucumber.
Try it as a side dish.

1. Mix all the ingredients and serve.
2. This can be made a day in advance, if you do this then
   don't add the lime juice, until just before serving.
3. Cut poppadom in 4, turn ends in to make a cone, fill
   with kachoomer and eat immediately.

Lassi (3 ways)

MEETHI LASSI (SWEET)
500ml natural plain yogurt
150ml cold water
1 tablespoon sugar
6-7 cubes of ice, crushed
3 tablespoons mango pulp

MEETHI LASSI (SWEET)
500ml natural plain yogurt
150ml cold water
3 tablespoons sugar
6-7 cubes of ice, crushed
1 teaspoon kewra water
   (optional)

NAMKEEN LASSI (SALTED)
500ml natural plain yogurt
150ml cold water
1 teaspoon cumin seeds,
   dry roasted and crushed
1 teaspoon salt or to taste
6-7 ice cubes, crushed ice

This drink is made from a combination of water and yogurt. It is designed to quench the thirst in a hot climate. Lassi can be sweet or salty.

1. Put the yogurt in a blender.
2. Add the water, sugar or salt or mango pulp, depending on which Lassi you are making.
3. Add the ice and kewra water if making sweet Lassi.
4. Blend on high speed for 2 minutes.

A hand blender can be used as an alternative to the blender.

Spicy Pomegranate Juice Drink

500ml Pomegranate juice
1 teaspoon cumin seeds,
   dry roasted and crushed
1 teaspoon chat masala
7-8 ice cubes, crushed
1 teaspoon fresh mint,
   crushed

1. Mix all the ingredients in a jug.
2. Serve in a tall glass.

Garam Masala

- tablespoon whole
  black peppercorns
- 2 teaspoons white
  cumin seeds
- 2 6cm sticks cinnamon
- 6 black cardamoms
- 1 tablespoon cloves
- 3 bay leaves
- 1 tablespoon
  coriander seeds
- ½ teaspoon nutmeg

You can buy and use many spices in Indian cooking, but you should always make your own garam masala. It's the secret ingredient to making fantastic Indian food. Garam masala means 'hot spices' and the variety of spices and aromas form the basis of most Indian dishes. The mixture is used in small amounts and generally added towards the end of the cooking time to enhance the flavour of the dish. It should be made in small quantities and stored in an airtight container.

1. Crush the cardamoms and dry roast all the spices on a low heat for 2 minutes.
2. Leave to cool and then grind the mixture into a very fine powder in a pestle and mortar or coffee grinder.
3. Store in an airtight container for upto one month.

About the author

Kumkum Chandra was born in Uttar Pradesh, India, and learned the techniques of cooking food in the region's distinctive style from an early age. She moved to England in 1971 with her husband, a general practitioner. Since then she has passed on her expertise by hosting a popular series of cookery classes as well as being a prolific writer. A devoted mother and grandmother, she produced all the recipes for this book at her favourite place – the kitchen of the family home in South Yorkshire.

Text: Kumkum Chandra and Karen Horsefield
Photographs: Charlie Staniland
Edited by: Martin Edwards, Chris Brierley, Victoria Philpott
Design: Steven Levers (www.stevenlevers.com), Paul Cocker

First published 2010 on behalf of Mrs K. Chandra

Published by:
RMC Books, Sheffield
Tel: (0114) 250 6300
www.regionalmagazine.co.uk

Mrs KUMKUM CHANDRA
7 Shoreham Avenue
Rotherham S60 3DB
S. Yorks. UK
tel-01709 370203
Email: kumkumesh@hotmail.com

Printed in the UK by Garnett Dickinson